Editor
Heather Douglas

Illustrator
Mark Mason

Cover Artist
Denise Bauer

Editor in Chief
Ina Massler Levin, M.A.

Creative Director
Karen J. Goldfluss, M.S. Ed.

Art Coordinator
Renée Christine Yates

Imaging
James Edward Grace

Publisher
Mary D. Smith, M.S. Ed.

BUILD WRITING SKILLS

Sounds to Letters

Includes Standards & Benchmarks

Relate reading to writing.

Understand how alphabetic symbols lead to the written form.

Construct meaning from sounds.

Establish meaning of sounds through writing.

mouse

Mm

Authors

Kathy Dickinson Crane, M. Ed. &
Kathleen Law, M. Ed.

Teacher Created Resources, Inc.
6421 Industry Way
Westminster, CA 92683
www.teachercreated.com

ISBN: 978-1-4206-3245-3

© 2010 Teacher Created Resources, Inc.
Made in U.S.A.

Teacher Created Resources

Table of Contents

Introduction

When writing is considered an important component of the reading process, amazing things can happen. Writing, after all, is the expression of things learned. It is an active process when students are allowed to discover, reflect, and create. Higher-order thinking skills are awakened as students analyze, synthesize, construct meaning, and make connections through use of the written word. Research has shown that reading and writing are co-dependent and the relationship thereof is that one cannot exist to full potential without the other; both reading and writing facilitate the other.

In order for students to optimize benefits from the writing process, effective writing strategies should be introduced and practiced. Writing strategies will allow students to expand the natural thinking process and transform that thinking into the written word.

Building Writing Skills—Sounds To Letters, if used in tandem with reputable reading and writing programs, will help establish crucial phonemic awareness and phonics skills in spoken language. These skills will allow students to gain confidence in the alphabetic symbols that produce sounds in the written form. As students participate in the activities and worksheets within this book, they will be able to construct meaning from sounds heard within words and establish meaning of those sounds through writing. This book maintains focus on the most common sounds of letters rather than alternate sounds. The letters are presented in the order of usefulness and frequency; furthermore, they are separated by visual and auditory similarity. Practice opportunities are provided as students write the visual representation for the initial sound within words as letter sounds are reviewed. Each activity within this book meets one or more of the McREL standards/benchmarks for the area of language arts.

Writing Standards

Each lesson in *Building Writing Skills—Sounds to Letters* meets one or more of the following language arts standards, which are used with permission from McREL (Copyright 2009, McREL, Mid-continent Research for Education and Learning. Telephone: 303-337-0990. Website: *www.mcrel.org*).

Standard	Pages
Uses the general skills and strategies of the writing process.	
• Knows that writing, including pictures, letters, and words, communicates meaning and information.	15, 23, 24, 30
• Uses drawings to express thoughts, feelings, and ideas.	10, 20
• Uses forms of emergent writing (e.g. scribble writing, random symbols, random letter-like marks) to represent ideas.	12, 18
• Dictates stories, poems, and personal narratives.	19, 25
• Uses emergent writing skills to write for a variety of purposes (e.g. to make lists, to send messages, to write stories) and to write in a variety of forms (e.g., journals, sign-in sheets, name cards, cards with words and pictures).	13, 14, 17, 22
• Uses knowledge of letters to write or copy familiar words, such as own name.	26, 29
• Uses writing tools, and materials (e.g., pencils, crayons, chalk, markers, rubber stamps, computers, paper, cardboard, chalkboard).	11, 16, 21, 27, 28, 47
Uses grammatical and mechanical conventions in written compositions.	
• Uses phonic knowledge to spell simple words.	5, 6-9, 31, 22-25, 36, 38-42, 43-46

Grab Bag Sounds

Objective
Identifying initial sounds.

Materials
- A bag or sack
- 20-30 objects

Preparation
Fill a sack, gift bag, or pillowcase with manipulatives and other items from your classroom or home. Seat the students on the floor or around a table. Place the bag of objects in front of you.

Directions
1. Have the first player grab an item out of the bag without peeking in the bag.

2. Identify the item for the player if necessary.

3. Ask the player to name the beginning sound of the item. (Naming the beginning letter is not necessary at this time.)

4. If the player correctly names the first sound of the object, he/she can keep the object until the end of the game.

5. If the student cannot name the initial sound, repeat the word, emphasizing the beginning sound slightly.

6. Identify the first sound with the student before he/she returns the object to the Grab Bag.

7. Continue around the group. Keep playing until the bag is empty.

8. Have the students count the number of collected items before returning them to the bag.

9. If time permits, play the game again. Challenge students to use their sense of touch to draw out new items for this game.

Pumpkin Patch Sound Game

Objective
Identifying initial sounds.

Materials
Pumpkin Patch sound cards.

Preparation
Cut out the 26 picture cards and 2 Pumpkin Buddy cards on pages 7 and 8. Color if desired. Copy 28 pumpkins on orange construction paper or cardstock using the pumpkins on page 9. Glue the picture cards and Pumpkin Buddies on the back of the pumpkins to make the Pumpkin Patch sound cards. Laminate pumpkins for durability.

Directions

1. Scatter the game cards on a table or floor, pumpkin-side up and picture-side down.

2. Inform the students that the pumpkin patch is filled with pumpkins ready to be picked.

3. Have Player A draw a pumpkin and turn it over.

4. Ask the player to name the beginning sound of the item. Identify the item for the player if necessary.

5. If the player correctly names the first sound of the picture, he/she keeps the pumpkin.

6. If the student cannot name the initial sound, repeat the word, emphasizing the beginning sound slightly. Identify the first sound with the student before he/she returns the pumpkin to the pumpkin patch.

7. If a player turns over a pumpkin with a Pumpkin Buddy on it, he/she keeps that pumpkin card. The player immediately gets another turn and should draw a card.

8. Next, have Player B draw a card and name the picture's beginning sound. Identify the picture for the player if necessary.

9. Continue taking turns until the players collect all of the pumpkins.

10. Have the students count the number of pumpkins before returning them to the pumpkin patch. The player with the most cards wins the game!

11. If time permits, mix up the pumpkins, place them picture-side down, and play the game again.

Pumpkin Patch Sound Game (cont.)

Pumpkin Patch Sound Game (cont.)

8

Pumpkin Patch Sound Game (cont.)

Name _____

S Letter and Sound

Directions

Ss makes the sound of /s/. Listen for the initial sound /s/ in each word. Then write the letter **s** where it belongs.

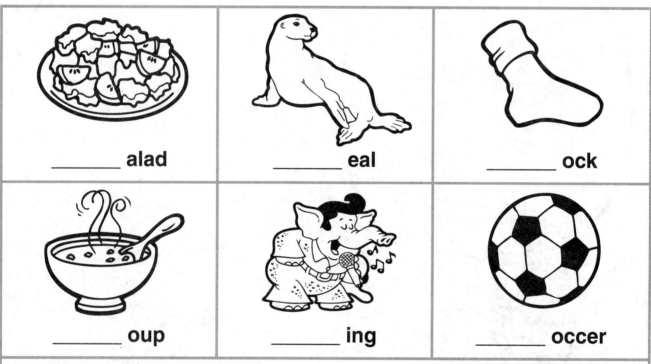

_____ alad	_____ eal	_____ ock
_____ oup	_____ ing	_____ occer

Directions

Draw a picture of something that begins with the letter **s**. Write the /s/ sound you hear at the beginning of the word and write any other sounds that you hear as you stretch the word out slowly.

     10

M Letter and Sound

Directions

Mm makes the sound of /m/. Say the name of each picture. If you hear the /m/ sound at the beginning of the word, write an uppercase **M** and a lowercase **m** on the line.

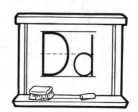

Name _____

D Letter and Sound

Directions

Dd makes the sound of /d/. Listen for the initial /d/ sound in each word. Write the letter **d** on each line to complete the word.

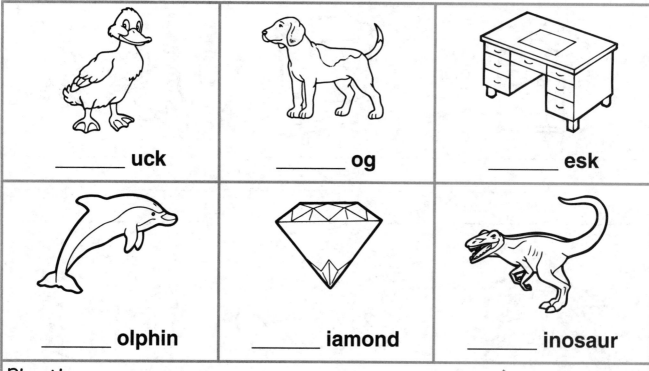

_____ **uck**   _____ **og**   _____ **esk**

_____ **olphin**   _____ **iamond**   _____ **inosaur**

Directions

Draw a picture of something that starts with the letter **d**. Tell someone a story about your picture. Write the letter **d** and any other letters that you hear when you stretch the word out slowly.

Name _____

P Letter and Sound

Directions

Pp makes the sound of /p/. Listen for the initial sound /p/ in each word. Then write the letter **p** where it belongs.

_____ **enguin**

_____ **ig**

_____ **ie**

_____ **ail**

_____ **ineapple**

_____ **umpkin**

Directions

Do you have any friends whose name begins with the letter **P**? Write those names.

Name _____

H Letter and Sound

Directions

Hh makes the sound of /h/. Heart begins with the /h/ sound. Say the name of each picture below. Circle the pictures that begin with the sound of **h**.

Choose one of the **Hh** pictures above and try to write its word. Put the letter **h** on the line below. Then stretch the word out slowly. Write any sounds that you hear.

_____

- -

_____

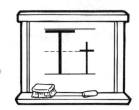

T Letter and Sound

Directions

Tt makes the sound of /t/. Listen for the initial sound /t/ in each word. Then write the letter **t** where it belongs.

_____ icket   _____ iger   _____ elephone

_____ urtle   _____ ree   _____ ornado

Directions

Draw a picture of something that begins with the sound of /t/. Write the beginning sound /t/, and then write any other sounds you hear in the word as you stretch the word out slowly.

Name _____

N Letter and Sound

Directions

Nn makes the sound of /n/. Say the name of each picture. If you hear the /n/ sound at the beginning of the word, write an uppercase **N** and a lowercase **n** under the picture.

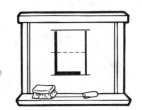

L Letter and Sound

Directions

Ll makes the sound of /l/. Listen to the initial sound in each picture below. Circle the word in each line that begins with the /l/ sound. Then, write one of the **Ll** words on the lines below.

- -

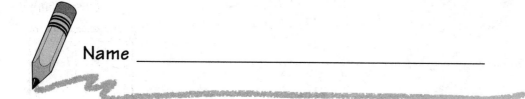

Name _____

B Letter and Sound

Directions

Bb makes the sound of /b/. Book begins with the /b/ sound. Draw four pictures beginning with the /b/ sound on the book pages below. Below each picture, write the letter **b** and any other sounds that you can hear.

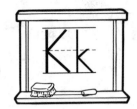

Name _____

K Letter and Sound

Directions

Kk makes the sound of /k/. Below are three pictures that begin with the /k/ sound. Name the pictures and then make up a story using all three words. Ask an adult to write your story for you.

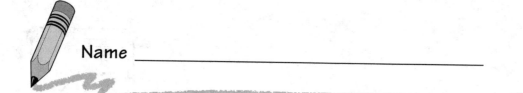

Name _____

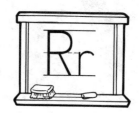

R Letter and Sound

Directions

Rr makes the sound of /r/. Listen for the /r/ sound at the beginning of each word. Write the letter **r** on the line.

_____ ope

_____ adio

_____ obot

_____ ing

_____ ocket

_____ attle

Directions

Draw a picture of something that starts with the letter **r**. Tell someone a story about your picture. Write the letter **r** and any other letters that you hear when you stretch the word out slowly.

Name _____

G Letter and Sound

Directions

Gg makes the sound of /g/. Trace the capital and lower case **Gg**'s below. Then draw a circle around all of the pictures that begin with the sound /g/.

Name _____

J Letter and Sound

Directions

Jj makes the sound of /j/. Jungle begins with the /j/ sound. Find the pictures in the jungle that begin with the /**j**/ sound. Color them.

Choose one of the **Jj** pictures above and try to write its word. Put the letter **j** on the line below. Then stretch the word out slowly. Write any sounds that you hear.

_____

- -

_____

Name _____

F Letter and Sound

Directions

The sound of **Ff** is /f/. Draw four pictures that begin with the /f/ sound and write the letter **f** in the speech bubble above each picture drawn.

Name _____

Z Letter and Sound

Directions

Zz makes the sound of /z/. Listen for the /z/ sound in each word. Write the letter **z** on each line.

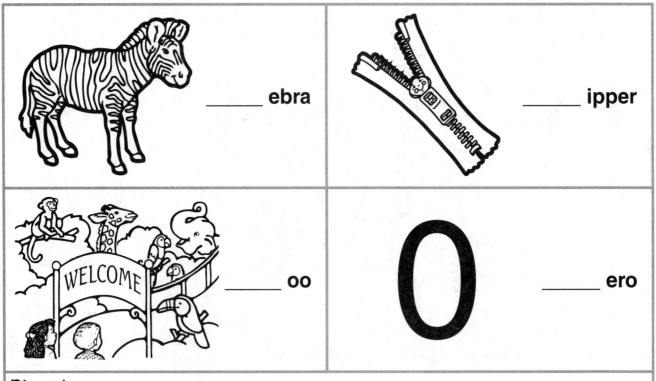

_____ **ebra**

_____ **ipper**

_____ **oo**

_____ **ero**

Directions

Draw a picture of a zoo. Write the word **zoo**. Write any other words that go with your picture by listening carefully to the sounds in the words.

W Letter and Sound

Directions

The sound of **Ww** is /w/. Use the letter **W** below to make an interesting picture. What is it? Ask an adult to write the words in the space below as you describe your picture.

Name _____

C Letter and Sound

Directions

Cc makes the hard /k/ sound and the soft /s/ sound. Crane and crate begin with the hard /k/ sound. Write the words **crane** and **crate** on the lines. Next, color each crate that contains an object that begins with the hard /k/ sound.

_____

crane

crate

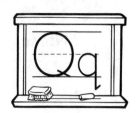

Q Letter and Sound

Directions

The word **quack** begins with the /kw/ sound as made by the letter **Qq**. Write a capital and lowercase **Qq** inside each speech bubble as the little duck quacks along.

Name _____

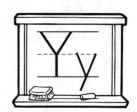

Y Letter and Sound

Directions

Yy makes the sound of /y/. Yo-yo begins with the /y/ sound. Listen as I name the pictures on this page. Find two pictures on each yo-yo that begin with the /y/ sound. Color them yellow. Then trace the letters **Yy** at the bottom of the page.

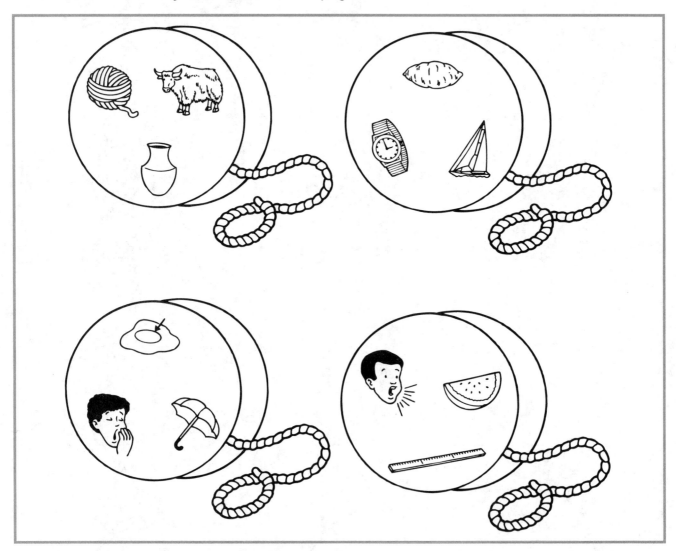

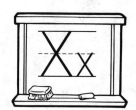

Name _____

X Letter and Sound

Directions

A fox was in a box! The letter **Xx** makes the sound of /ks/. Draw a picture of a fox in the box and then write the two words **fox** and **box** below.

fox

box

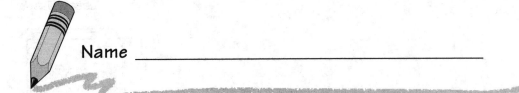

Name _____

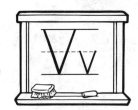

V Letter and Sound

Directions

Vv makes the sound of /v/. The words below all begin with the /v/ sound. Choose two words and draw pictures of them. Write about your pictures by copying the words or listening for sounds and writing their letters.

vase	vegetables	vest	volcano
vulture	valentine	van	vacuum

30

Name _____

The Vowels—Letters and Sounds

Directions

The pictures below begin with a vowel. Say the name of the picture and write the missing vowel sound at the beginning of each word.

_pple

_gg

_guana

_strich

_ncle

_nt

_nch

_mpire

_ctopus

Ocean Adventure Vowel Game

Objective

Connecting vowel sounds to letters.

Materials

Ocean Adventure game board, Ocean Adventure picture cards, and game markers.

Preparation

Copy the Ocean Adventure game board and picture cards found on pages 33, 34, and 35 onto cardstock. Color if desired and laminate for durability. Cut the picture cards apart.

Directions

1. Lay the game board in the center of the group. Place the picture cards face down in the middle of the board.

2. Player A draws a vowel picture card and identifies the beginning vowel sound. (The name of the picture is on the card. Read it to the player if he/she does not recognize the picture.)

3. If the sound is correctly identified, Player A may move his/her game piece to the first letter matching that sound.

4. If the beginning sound is not identified or produced correctly, the player's turn is over.

5. Set the card in a discard pile off of the game board.

6. Player B follows the same steps of drawing a card, identifying the beginning sound, then moving to the first letter that goes with the sound.

7. Play always moves forward; if there is not a vowel ahead of the game marker that matches the sound, the play may go directly to FINISH.

8. When all cards are in the discard pile, mix them up, and place them face down on the treasure chest.

9. Continue playing until all players reach the octopus and FINISH.

10. If time permits, mix up the picture cards and begin again.

Ocean Adventure Vowel Game (cont.)

a	o	u	e	i	a	i
i						e
a						o
o						u
a						a
u						e
e						i
i						i
o						e
e		FINISH				
e	u	o	i	e	a	START

Ocean Adventure Vowel Game (cont.)

apple	ant	elephant
exit	igloo	alligator
apron	egg	eagle
iguana	astronaut	angel
elevator	eating	infant

34

Ocean Adventure Vowel Game (cont.)

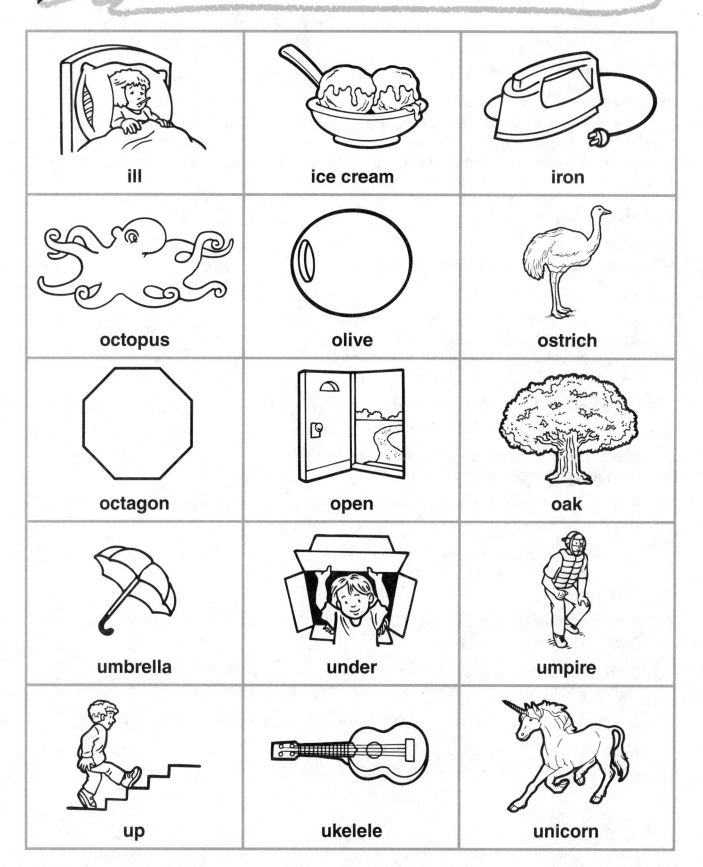

ill	ice cream	iron
octopus	olive	ostrich
octagon	open	oak
umbrella	under	umpire
up	ukelele	unicorn

Letter and Sound Relay

Objective
Connecting sounds to letters.

Preparation
Make a set of letter floor tiles using 26 pieces of construction paper or cardstock. Write one letter of the alphabet on each page and laminate for durability. Next, find an object for each letter of the alphabet. The object should begin with the letter's sound. The picture cards found on pages 7 and 8 may be substituted for the objects if preferred.

Materials
- Letter floor tiles
- A basket of 26 objects or picture cards.

Directions

1. Lay the 26 letter tiles in alphabetical order on the floor. If possible, choose a large area such as a gym or an outside area to permit running during this game.

2. Place the 26 objects or picture cards in a basket. Set them a short distance from the letters.

3. Divide the students into two teams and assign one player on each team to begin.

4. Have Player A from each team walk or run (if the area is large enough) to the basket and choose one object.

5. When each player returns, he/she must name the initial sound of the object and match it to its corresponding letter. Teammates may assist with sound and letter identification if necessary.

6. If the object is placed on its correct letter, Player B for the team may walk (or run) to the basket and choose an object.

7. If the object is not placed on the correct letter, provide assistance so the team can place it on the right floor tile. Player B may then go to the basket to pick up another object.

8. Continue playing until all of the objects have been placed on the correct letter tiles.

9. Mix up the items and begin again. Encourage players to choose different items in order to practice identifying other letters and sounds.

Letter and Sound Relay (cont.)

Below are examples of what you can use as objects or pictures of objects to represent each letter.

apple	farm	kitchen	quilt	umbrella
alligator	five	key	quill	ukulele
ankle	football	lion	quartz	volcano
anteater	golf ball	leg	quicksand	vacuum
ball	gorilla	lamb	quarter	vulture
bat	girl	lake	quail	van
bubble	garden	milk	rope	vest
bug	grass	mouse	radio	walrus
bingo	gate	monkey	robot	watch
butterfly	glasses	mountain	ring	wink
cat	heart	mask	rocket	whisper
camera	hook	nest	rattle	x-ray
coin	hippo	nut	rainbow	xylophone
crane	horse	nose	rabbit	(fo)x
crab	harp	number	soup	(bo)x
carrot	hat	necklace	sock	yak
dog	helmet	nails	shoe	yo-yo
dough	house	newspaper	seal	yarn
dollar	igloo	octopus	soccer	yardstick
dimple	iguana	ostrich	sing	yam
duck	inch	octagon	ticket	yolk
diamond	ice	penguin	tea	yawn
dinosaur	juice	pig	tiger	zipper
dolphin	jelly beans	pie	turtle	zero
desk	jeep	pail	tree	zebra
elephant	jacket	pineapple	tornado	zoo
eagle	jug	pumpkin	telephone	
egg	jam or jelly	pinky	tiger	
fork	kite	queen	umpire	
family	king	quack	uncle	

Beary Fun Lotto

Objective
Matching sounds to letters.

Preparation
Copy the player and sound cards found on pages 39-41 onto card stock. Laminate for durability, and cut apart. Place the sound cards into a box that has been decorated to look like a bear cave.

Materials
- player cards
- sound cards
- bear cave
- a bowl of markers for each student such as bear counters, beans, buttons, etc.
- a pencil and a writing worksheet for each student.

Directions
1. Each player chooses a player card and a cup filled with bingo markers.

2. Each player will take a turn drawing a sound card from the bear cave. Player A begins.

3. When a card is drawn, Player A will name the picture on the card and identify the beginning sound. For example, if the card shows a picture of an apple, the player will exaggerate the beginning sound, /a/-/a/-/a/. The player then states that the letter is **a**!

4. Then, Player A looks at his/her player card and places a marker on the bear that is naming that letter. If there is not a letter matching the sound, the play will simply pass to the next player. (*For variation of game, other players may cover letters when it is not their turn.*)

5. The next player, Player B, then draws a picture card out of the bear cave and repeats steps 3 and 4.

6. Play continues until one player fills his/her player card with bingo markers. At that time, that player yells, *GROWL*!

7. When *GROWL* is called, all players must run away from the bears. In order to do so, each player must write the lowercase alphabet letters on the worksheet. As each player writes his/her last letter, **z**, they call, "*Made-it, I'm safe!*"

Variation: Cut player cards in half so each student has nine letters.

Beary Fun Lotto (cont.)

l	n	p
r	t	v
x	z	q
m	n	q
s	u	w
y	b	e

Beary Fun Lotto (cont.)

a	c	e
g	i	t
m	o	v
s	u	w
y	b	d
f	h	j

Beary Fun Lotto (cont.)

Beary Fun Lotto *(cont.)*

a b c d e f g h i j k l m n o p q r s t u v w x y z

Instructions:

Write all of your lowercase letters from a–z. When you have reached **z**, you are safely home! (But remember, all letters must be lowercase to beat the bear home!)

Score Twenty-Four

Objective

Identifying beginning sounds of words and writing the visual representation of that sound.

Materials

- mystery box
- a basket for discard
- football cards
- scoring sheet and pencil for each player

Preparation

1. Use an old rectangular tissue box as a mystery box. Remove plastic from the top slot but keep the hole intact. Students will draw and return cards into the top slot of the box.

2. Copy the football cards found on page 44-46 onto sturdy tag and laminate for durability. Place cards inside of mystery box in the center of the table.

3. Create a scoring sheet by making 24 boxes on a page.

4. Pass each student a scoring sheet and a pencil

Directions

(4–5 players)

1. Player A will draw a card from the mystery box, name the picture on the card and identify its beginning sound. The player will then write the letter that represents that sound in the top left square of his/her worksheet. The player then places the card into a discard basket. **Note:** *If all footballs are played, return to mystery box for replay.*

2. Going around the table in a clockwise manner, each player will take a turn accordingly. The players will write the letters in a left to right manner filling each square.

3. If a player draws a fumble, the play goes immediately to the next player. The fumble card is returned to the mystery box rather than the discard basket.

4. Continue around the table until the first player scores 24!

Note: *To keep the game at a fast pace, have the next player draw a card as soon as the previous player identifies his/her beginning sound and begins to write his/her letter.*

Score Twenty-Four (cont.)

44 ©Teacher Created Resources, Inc.

Score Twenty-Four (cont.)

Score Twenty-Four (cont.)

(seahorse)	(turtle)	(yo-yo)
(zipper)	(bucket)	(clown)
(girl kicking)	(fan)	(goat)
(heart)	(pickle)	(beans)
(robot)	(mummy)	(hamburger)
Fumble	Fumble	Fumble
Fumble	Fumble	Fumble

Handwriting Practice

Directions

Trace each capital and lowercase letter with a crayon or pencil.

A a	B b	C c	D d
E e	F f	G g	H h
I i	J j	K k	L l
M m	N n	O o	P p
Q q	R r	S s	T t
U u	V v	W w	
X x	Y y	Z z	

Answer Key

Page 7-8

apple /a/, butterfly /b/, crayon /k/, dog /d/, elephant /e/, fork /f/, glasses /g/, house /h/, igloo /i/, jar /j/, kite /k/, leaf /l/, moon /m/, nest /n/, orange /o/, pear /p/, queen /kw/, robot /r/, sailboat /s/, tree /t/, unicorn /u/, violin /v/, whale /w/, x-ray /x/, yo-yo /y/, zebra /z/

Page 11

Write the letter m under the picture for 1, 3, 4, 5, 7 and 9

Page 14

Circle the following: house, hook, helmet, horse, hippo, harp, hand, hat

Page 16

Write the letter n under the pictures for 1, 2, 4, 6, 7, 9, 11 and 12

Page 17

Circle the following: lion, leg, lamb

Page 21

Circle the following: golf, gorilla, girl, goose, grass, gate, garden

Page 22

Circle the following: jar, jack-in-the-box, jaguar, jacket, jug, jellybeans, jeep, juice

Page 26

Color the following: crab, canoe, camera, carrots, computer, car

Page 28

Color the following: yak, yarn, yacht, yam, yawn, yoke, yardstick, yelling

Page 31

Write the initial letters: a, e, i, o, u, a i, u, o

Page 41

elephant /e/, fish /f/, gum /g/, hat /h/, iguana /i/, juice /j/, lemon /l/, milk /m/, nut /n/, ostrich /o/, pear /p/, quilt /kw/, robot /r/, sailboat /s/, tree /t/, unicorn /u/, bear /b/, ant /a/, cat /k/, violin /v/, whale /wh/, yak /y/, zebra /z/

Page 44-46

swing /sw/, television /t/, violin /v/, watermelon /w/, yak /y/, zebra /z/, apple /a/, bear /b/, cat /k/, elephant /e/, fish /f/, grape /g/, hat /h/, jacket /j/, kangaroo /k/, lion /l/, monkey /m/, nut /n/, pumpkin /p/, queen /kw/, rabbit /r/